to

_____

from

_____

To Amelia, Harriet, Lucie
and Jay A.A.

Text by Lois Rock
Illustrations copyright © 2003 Alex Ayliffe
This edition copyright © 2006 Lion Hudson

The moral rights of the author and illustrator
have been asserted

A Lion Children's Book
an imprint of
Lion Hudson plc
Mayfield House, 256 Banbury Road,
Oxford OX2 7DH, England
www.lionhudson.com
ISBN-13: 978-0-7459-6005-0
ISBN-10: 0-7459-6005-7

First edition 2003
This edition 2006
1 3 5 7 9 10 8 6 4 2 0

A catalogue record for this book is available
from the British Library

Typeset in 22/30 Baskerville BT
Printed and bound in Hong Kong

my very first
Bible

Words by
Lois Rock

Pictures by
Alex Ayliffe

LION
CHILDREN'S

Contents

Old Testament

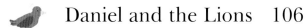

New Testament

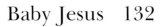

Dear God,
These are Bible stories.
Help me to listen.

Dear God,
These are Bible stories.
Help me to imagine.

Dear God,
These are Bible stories.
Help me to understand.

Old
Testament

In the Beginning

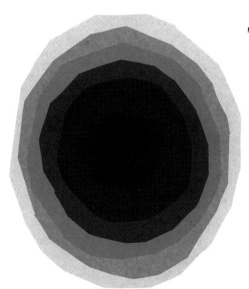

Think of the dark.
Make it darker.
Think of the
darkest dark.

In the beginning,
there was nothing
but dark.

Then God spoke:
"Let there be light."

And the very first light shone
brightly.

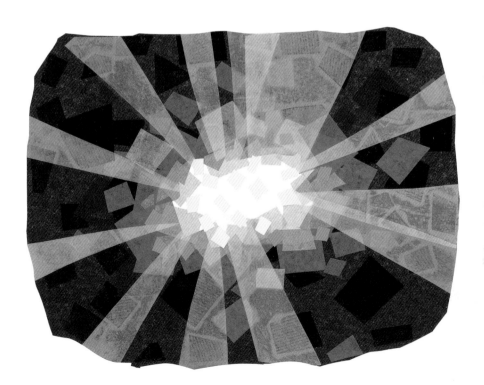

God spread the sky
wide above the ocean,
and folded the land to
make hills and valleys.

God covered the earth with
plants: grasses and flowers,
vegetables and trees.

The sun shone in the
daytime, and the moon
and stars waited for their
turn in the night-time.

God made all the creatures.

Birds flew in the sky.

Fish swam in the seas.

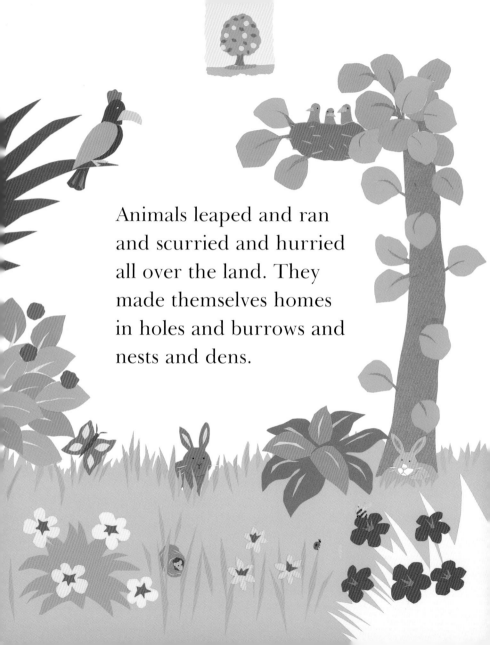

Animals leaped and ran
and scurried and hurried
all over the land. They
made themselves homes
in holes and burrows and
nests and dens.

Then God made people—man and woman. "Welcome," said God. "You are my friends, and I want you to be safe and happy. Take care of the good world I have made for you.

"Never choose to know about bad things: they will only make you sad."

Everything was perfect...

Then, one day, people
wanted to find out about
bad things as well as good
things.

The snake whispered what to
do: they ate some fruit God
had told them not to eat.

Their world changed.

They were no longer good friends with God.

Instead, they felt all alone in an unkind world. They had to work very hard for everything they needed.

"Can things ever be put right
again?" they wondered. People have
been wondering ever since.

Noah and the Ark

Long ago, God looked down to see the world.

God had made a good world. Now people were spoiling it.

They were always fighting.

"I'm sorry I ever made the world," said God. "I shall wash it away."

God saw that there was one good man: Noah.

"I want you to build a big boat," said God to Noah. "It will be called the ark."

Noah was puzzled.

"There is going to be a flood," said God. "You must take your family on the ark, to keep them safe."

Noah began to build.

God said, "Noah, you must also take animals onto the ark. You must take a father and a mother of every kind of animal."

Noah and his family were
very busy doing as God
wanted.

Then it rained and rained.
The whole world was flooded.

The ark floated on the flood
water for days and days and
days.

At last, the rain stopped. The water started to go down.

Bump! Noah's ark hit the top of a mountain and got stuck there.

Noah let out a raven. It flew and flew and kept on flying.

Noah let out a dove.
The first time, it soon
flew back.

The second time, it came
back with an olive branch
in its beak. The third time,
it flew away.

"It must have found land,"
said Noah.

Soon the land was dry. Noah let everyone out of the ark. The animals hurried away to make new homes.

"Thank you, God, for keeping us safe," said Noah.

God was pleased. "Look," said God, "there is my rainbow in the sky. It is a promise that I will keep the whole world safe forever."

Grandfather Abraham

Long ago lived a man named Abram. His family was very rich.

They had sheep and goats
and cattle and donkeys
and camels.

One day, God
spoke to Abram.

"Abram, I want you to leave your father's home and go to a new land.

"I have chosen you to be the great-great-great-grandfather of many people. You and your family will bring my blessing to all the world."

Abram believed that what God said was true. He set out at once with his wife, Sarai, his family and his animals.

They reached the land
of Canaan. "You can make
your home here," said God.

It was a good land, but Abram
had to find grass for his
animals.

They had to keep on moving from place to place. Life was often hard. Sometimes it made them sad.

"I wonder if what God said is really true," thought Abram.

One dark night, God spoke to Abram
again. "Look up at the stars in the
sky... too many to count," said God.
"You will be the great-great-great-
grandfather of many people... too
many to count."

Abram believed that what God said
was true.

"I am going to give you and Sarai new names," said God. "You will be Abraham: Great-great-great-grandfather Abraham.

"Your wife will be Sarah: Great-great-great-grandmother Sarah."

Many years passed. Abraham
and Sarah still had no children.

Abraham sighed. "Can I still
believe that what God said will
come true?" he said.

Sarah looked at other people's children and sighed. "I find it hard to believe that what God said is true," she said.

Then, at last, Sarah and Abraham had a baby. They called him Isaac.

"God has made me so happy I can laugh again," said Sarah. And she knew that one day she was going to be the great-great-great-grandmother of many people.

"This is a time to be happy," said Abraham. "Now we know that what God says *is* true."

He was sure that one day he was going to be the great-great-great-grandfather of many people.

Joseph and His Dream

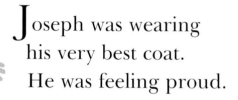

Joseph was wearing his very best coat. He was feeling proud.

His great-grandfather was Abraham.

His grandfather was Isaac.

His father was Jacob.

Jacob had given Joseph the wonderful coat.
It was better than anything he had given to
Joseph's older brothers.

Joseph believed he was very, very important.

His older brothers were very, very jealous.

One day, the brothers were out looking after their father's goats and sheep. Jacob sent Joseph to check that everything was all right.

The brothers grabbed him. They took his coat. Then they saw some merchants passing nearby. They sold Joseph to the men.

The men took Joseph to a place called Egypt.

The brothers told their father, Jacob, that Joseph was dead. Jacob was very sad.

In Egypt, Joseph was sold as a slave. He had to work very hard. Then someone told a lie about Joseph and he went to prison.

Nobody there cared about Joseph. But God helped Joseph understand dreams and explain their meaning.

One day, the great king of
Egypt had a strange dream.
Someone sent for Joseph.

Joseph understood the king's dream:

"There are going to be seven years of good harvests and seven years of bad harvests," he explained. "Find someone wise to keep grain from the good harvests; it will feed the people when the harvests are bad."

The king chose Joseph.
He became very rich and
very important.

The bad years came. Joseph was in charge of using the grain in the barns.

From far away came ten hungry people.

They bowed down to the important man in charge and asked to buy food.

Joseph knew these people were his brothers, but they didn't know who he was.

Was Joseph going to punish them, or was he going to be kind?

Joseph really wanted to see his one younger brother, Benjamin. He made the others go to fetch him.

Then, at last, Joseph told the brothers who he was. "God was in charge of everything that happened," he said. "I was sent to Egypt so that I could rescue you now."

Joseph invited all his family
to come and live in Egypt.
There they made their home.

Moses and
the King

When Miriam was a little girl, she liked to dance and play the tambourine. She also liked to listen to stories with her little brother, Aaron.

They liked the story of Great-great-ever-so-many-greats Grandfather Abraham.

"God promised Abraham a land of our own," said Miriam's mother. "Our family came to Egypt many years ago to find food here. Now the king of Egypt has made us slaves.

"Now the king wants our baby boys killed," she sobbed.

"What about my new baby brother?" Miriam asked.

They hid him in a basket among the reeds.

Miriam saw the princess of Egypt come and find the baby.

"I shall keep him safe," said the princess. "I shall call him Moses. But who will take care of him?"

Miriam stepped forward. "I can find someone to take care of the baby," she said. She fetched her mother.

When he was older Moses grew up as a prince, but he knew he was one of the slave people.

One day, he got into a bad fight for trying to help a slave, and he had to run away.

He became a shepherd.

In the desert, Moses saw a strange thing: a bush on fire that wasn't burning. He heard God speaking: "Go back to Egypt, Moses, and tell that king to let my people go. Your brother will help you."

Together Moses and Aaron
went to see the king.

"I will not let your
people go," he told
them.

They asked over and over again, but the king always said, "NO!"

"God wants you to let our people go," said Aaron and Moses. "If you don't, there will be trouble."

There was lots of
trouble: frogs, then
flies, then locusts—
everywhere!

There were all sorts
of horrible things.

At last, the king told Moses and
Aaron to come and see him.
"Hurry up and go!" he said.

God helped everyone escape.
They set out for the land God had
promised to Great-great-ever-so-
many-greats Grandfather Abraham.

Moses and Aaron led the way.

Miriam played her tambourine and danced, just like she used to when she was little.

Brave Joshua

When the way ahead is scary, who goes first?

Someone who is strong and brave.

Someone like Joshua.

As Moses led his people to
the land God had promised
them, he noticed Joshua.

As Moses told the people God's laws, he noticed that Joshua always listened.

"You must love God most of all, and you must love others as you love yourself," said Moses.

Joshua always obeyed and tried
to help others to do the same.

The people wandered for
many years on the way to the
new land. Moses grew old.

He chose Joshua to lead the
people into the new land.
Joshua stood on the bank
of the River Jordan, on the
edge of the new land.

"Teach the people to obey my laws," said God, "and I will help you make the land your home."

The first place the people came to was the city
of Jericho. It had walls all around it. Strong
soldiers stood on guard.

God told Joshua what to do.

Joshua told the people to march around the city. One day they marched. Two days they marched. Three days they marched. Four days they marched. Five days they marched. Six days they marched. Seven days they marched, and then…

The priests blew
their trumpets.

All the people
shouted.

The walls of
Jericho fell down.

The people entered the city.

It was the first step towards
making the land a home.

When the land was theirs,
Joshua made sure that
everyone had a share.

Then he asked everyone to come to
a great meeting.

"We are at home in the land God has
given us," he said. "I have decided
that I will always live as God wants:
I will love God most of all,
and I will love others as
much as I love myself.
What will you do?"

"We will live as
God wants,"
said the
people.

David and
His Song

When he was very
little, David liked
to throw stones.

When he was
bigger, he learned
to throw them with
a sling.

He was good
at throwing—he
could hit what
he wanted.

At night, his mother told him
about God.

She taught him to say
thank-you prayers to God
for everything he had
and for all the things
he could do.

When David was a bit older, his job was looking after the sheep.

He threw stones to scare away wild animals.

David was never scared. He sang
thank-you songs to God for
everything he had and
for all the things he
could do.

One day, David went to visit his big brothers. They were soldiers.

They were fighting fierce enemies.

One was a giant. He wore shiny battle clothes and had a big spear. "I am Goliath," roared the giant. "If anyone can beat me, then my army will go away! Who dares to try?"

"I dare," said David. For David believed that God was always with him and would help him win.

"You're too little,"
said his brothers.

"You're too little,"
said his king.

"But I can fight lions and
bears and wolves, and I know
God is with me," said David.

"Take care," they warned.

David went out.

He picked up
five stones.

"How dare you fight
me like that!" said the
giant.

"I dare because God is with me,"
said David. He put a stone in his
sling.

He threw.

The giant fell.

David grew up to be the next king of
his people. He still sang thank-you
songs to God for everything he had
and for all he could do.

"Dear God, you are my shepherd,
You give me all I need—
My food, my drink, a place to rest,
Yes, you are good indeed.

When all the world seems gloomy
And scary things are near,
You always take good care of me
And so I need not fear.

You've given me so many things,
And everyone can see
The special loving kindness
You always show to me."

Jonah and the Whale

Jonah was feeling grumpy.

"I'm a prophet," he was thinking. "My job is to tell our people about our God—the God who loves us.

"Now God wants me to go and visit our worst enemies—our enemies in Nineveh. And why?

"BECAUSE GOD WANTS TO
FORGIVE THEM FOR ALL
THE BAD THINGS THEY DO!

"Well, I won't."

Jonah ran down to the sea.
He got on a boat. It was
going to take him far away
from Nineveh.

Then God sent a storm.

"It's all my fault," wailed Jonah to the sailors. "Throw me overboard, or the storm will sink us all." So they did.

The storm stopped. The sailors on the boat were safe.

Jonah sank deep down in the
sea, where a great big fish
came and swallowed him up.

Jonah knew that God had sent the fish.

"Help me, help me!" he prayed.

The fish spat Jonah
onto dry land.

Once again God told Jonah to go to Nineveh.
At last he went.

"Here is a message
from God!" he cried.
"Stop doing bad
things. If you don't,
terrible things will
happen."

The king heard the news.

"Everyone, stop being bad," he ordered.

God forgave everyone. That made Jonah very grumpy indeed.

He went and made himself a little
shelter. He sat in it and sulked.

"Why are you cross?" asked God.

"The people of Nineveh did bad
things," said Jonah. "You shouldn't
have been kind to them."

God made a lovely plant
grow over Jonah's shelter.

It gave cool shade.

 The next day, God sent a worm to eat the plant, and it died.

The sun was hot. The wind was hotter. Jonah was grumpier than ever.

"Why are you cross?" asked God. "I'm cross about my poor plant," said Jonah.

"Are you feeling sorry for a plant?"
said God. "Well, I'm feeling sorry for
all the people of Nineveh and all their
animals. Even if they were once bad,
I still love them."

Daniel and
the Lions

Daniel always did what
he believed was right.

He always said prayers
to God.

He always obeyed God.

Daniel did what he believed was right even when everything else went wrong.

One sad day, the great-great-great-ever-so-many-great-grandchildren of Abraham lost a fight against enemy soldiers.

Daniel was one of the people taken far away. He went to Babylon.

Everything was going wrong.

Daniel went on doing what
he believed was right.

He always followed God's laws.

The king of Babylon saw that
Daniel was a good man. He gave
him a very important job.

That made other
people very jealous.

They went to see the king.

"O king," they said. "You are so great and wonderful. Make a law that says you will punish anyone who treats anyone else as more important than you."

"Good idea," said the king.

"Say that anyone who disobeys will be thrown into a pit of lions," said the men.

"Good idea," said the king.

Daniel knew that everything was going wrong.

He still did what he believed was right. He still said prayers to God. He still obeyed God.

The men came to spy on him. They saw what he was doing.

Then they went and told the king.

"Daniel is praying to his God. He thinks his God is greater than you."

The king was sad. Now he must punish Daniel.

Daniel was
thrown into a pit
of hungry lions.

Everything was going wrong.

Daniel still did what he
believed was right.

He still said prayers to God.

He still obeyed God.

The next morning, the king came to see what had happened.

Daniel was alive. God had not let the lions hurt him.

"Hooray!" said the king. "I shall
make a law that everyone must respect
Daniel's God. He will be safe, and
those bad men will be punished."

Everything was going right, and Daniel
still did what he believed was right.

Nehemiah's Prayers

Nehemiah worked in the palace of the emperor of Persia. One day he was feeling sad.

"Why do you look so sad?" asked the emperor.

Nehemiah said a prayer to God. Then he answered, "My real homeland is far away. Our great city was knocked down in a fight. Now that the fight is over, my people want to go back and build it up."

The emperor let Nehemiah go to help mend the city— the great city of Jerusalem, in the homeland of the great-great-great-ever-so-many-great-grandchildren of Abraham.

Nehemiah rode around the city on a donkey, looking at the broken walls.

Then he met with all the people.

"God has helped me get here," he said. "I want to help mend the city."

"Let's all mend it," the people said.

Everybody worked,
and the walls
began to grow...

and grow...

Some other people came
to watch. "You'll
never mend a city
as broken down
as this," they
laughed.

Nehemiah said a prayer to God. Then he spoke to the people. "Don't worry about what others think," he said.

Next Nehemiah heard that some people were planning to spoil all the work.

"Don't be afraid," said Nehemiah. "God will help us."

He told half the people to keep on building. The other half kept watch with swords and spears—they were ready to protect the builders.

At last the work was done. Everyone came to a great meeting.

A priest read out the laws God had given Moses: "Love God most of all, and love others as you love yourself."

Then everyone said a prayer:

"God, you made the world.
You chose Abraham to be the
great-grandfather of our people.
You chose Moses to lead us to freedom.
You took us to a homeland.
You gave us good laws.
We have sometimes disobeyed you
and made everything go wrong.
We are sorry, and we promise now
to keep your laws."

Nehemiah was happy. God
had answered all his prayers.

Tell me the stories of Jesus
  I love to hear;
things I would ask him to tell
  me if he were here;
scenes by the wayside, tales
  of the sea,
stories of Jesus, tell them to me.

A children's hymn

New Testament

Baby Jesus

In the little town of Nazareth lived a young woman named Mary. She was looking forward to getting married.

One day, an angel came to visit her.

"Don't be afraid," said the angel.

"God has chosen
you for something very
special. You are going to
have a baby: God's own
Son. You must call him Jesus.
He will bring God's blessings to the
world."

Mary was very surprised but she
agreed. "I will do as God
wants," she said.

Mary was looking forward to marrying Joseph. But when Joseph heard Mary's news, he was worried.

Then an angel spoke to him in a dream. "Take care of Mary," said the angel. "Her baby is God's own Son. He will bring God's blessings to all the world."

Joseph was very puzzled, but he said
he would take care of Mary.

And together they went to
take part in a great counting
of people that was being
done. They went to
Bethlehem.

The town was very
busy. The only place to
stay was in a room full
of animals.

There, Mary's baby was born. Mary
wrapped him in swaddling clothes.
She laid him to sleep in a manger.

Out in the fields nearby, shepherds were watching their sheep. An angel appeared.

"Do not be afraid," said the angel. "Tonight, in Bethlehem, a baby has been born: God's special king, who will bring God's blessings to the world."

Then all the angels sang
together for joy.

The shepherds went to
Bethlehem.

They found Mary and the baby,
just as the angel had said.

Far away, wise men saw a special star in the night sky.

"It is a sign that a new king has been born," they said. "We must go and find him."

The star led them to the place
where Jesus was.

They brought him gifts: gold,
frankincense and myrrh.

Mary smiled. The gifts for Jesus were gifts for a king.

"The king who will bring God's blessings to the world," she said to herself.

Jesus Grows Up

Jesus grew up in Nazareth.

He learned the old stories: about Noah and Abraham and many others.

He learned about Moses and the
laws God had given him: "Love God
most of all, and love others as you
love yourself."

Every year, the
people remembered
the story of Moses
and the great escape
from Egypt. They
held a special festival
called Passover.

The best place to be at festival time
was the big city of Jerusalem. When
Jesus was twelve, he went with Mary
and Joseph and lots of people from
Nazareth.

The most important part of the
festival took place in the Temple.

All around, wise teachers sat and
talked about the old stories and the
laws God had given Moses.

After the festival, everyone from
Nazareth set off for home.

They had gone some way when Mary
thought, "Where is Jesus? I haven't
seen him all day."

No one had seen him.

Mary and Joseph rushed
back to Jerusalem.

At last they found Jesus.
He was sitting with the wise
teachers, talking about the old
stories and the laws.

"Why are you here?" asked
Mary. "We have been so
worried about you."

"Why?" said Jesus. "Didn't
you know that I had to be
in my Father's house?"

Mary didn't really understand.
She just wanted Jesus to be safe.

Then Jesus went back home. He
grew to be a man. He was a good
son to his parents.
He learned the
kind of work
that Joseph did.

Then, one day, he went off
to begin a new kind of work.

Jesus became a wise teacher.
He helped people understand
the old stories and the laws.
He wanted people to
understand what God
is like.

He wanted people to know
how much God loves them.

Jesus and His Friends

Jesus the wise teacher told people about God. He told people that God loves them and welcomes them as friends.

"Follow me," said Jesus. "Come and listen to what I have to say, and help spread the news."

"We will come," said the fishermen. They left their fishing nets and their boat. They followed Jesus.

"I will come," said the tax collector. He left his money and his greedy friends to follow Jesus.

"I will come," said the rich lady, "for he is showing people the loving way to live, and I want to help."

There were other women,
too, who followed Jesus:
some rich and some poor.

"We will follow Jesus," said the mother and the father, "for our little girl was dead…"

"But Jesus made me as alive as can be," danced the little girl.

Other people danced too:
people who had not been
able to walk until Jesus
made them well.

The sparrows
twittered happily
in the olive trees.

They swooped
close to Jesus.

They dared to hop
near his feet.

Something seemed to tell
them that Jesus noticed them
and loved them as well.

Some mothers came to Jesus. "We want Jesus to say a prayer for our children," they said.

"Sorry," said some of his
friends. "He's too busy."

"I am not too busy," said
Jesus. "I welcome children.
For God welcomes children.

"So all of my friends must welcome little children and love them."

The Hole
in the Roof

Many people came to
see Jesus and to listen
to what he had to say.
Some of the people were
teachers. They were not
all sure that they liked
Jesus' teaching.

One day, Jesus was talking
to people inside a house.
It was very crowded.

Yet more people
came to see Jesus.

"We have heard he can heal people
by miracles," they said. "Our friend
cannot walk. We are carrying him
here on his sleeping mat so Jesus
can heal him."

There was a problem:
they could not even get
into the house.

On the outside of the house,
steps led up to the flat roof.

The men took their
friend up onto the roof.

172

They made a hole in the roof
and let the man down on ropes,

right in front of Jesus.

"All the bad that is in you has
been forgiven," said Jesus with
a smile.

"He can't say that!" said some of the wise teachers to each other. "Only God can say that."

Jesus smiled. He wanted
people to understand that God
loves people, that God forgives
people, that God wants to
make people well, and that
God wants to be friends with
people.

He said to the man,
"Get up and walk."

The man got up and
walked home. He even
carried his sleeping mat.

"God has done wonderful
things for me," he said to
his friends.

The Boat in the Storm

Jesus was very busy. There always seemed to be a lot of people wanting to see him.

One evening, he said to his close friends, "Come, let's go in our boat across to the other side of the lake."

His friends got into the boat with him.

In the boat, Jesus soon fell asleep.

Suddenly a strong wind began
to blow.

The waves began to crash
against the sides of the boat.

The waves began to
spill into the boat.

"Wake up and help us,"
shouted Jesus' friends. "We
are going to sink with the
boat!"

185

Jesus stood up.

"Be quiet," he said to the waves.
"Be still," he said to the wind.

Then everything was calm.
Everything that was dark
and dangerous and scary
just went away.

The day came, bright and
clear.

"What made you so scared?"
asked Jesus. "Don't you believe
in God?"

Jesus' friends knew they were
safe, but they were more
scared than ever.

"Who is our friend Jesus?"
they asked each other. "Who
can he be? Even the wind and
waves obey him."

The Good Samaritan

A teacher once came and asked Jesus a question: "What is the right way to live?"

Jesus asked him a question: "You are a teacher. What do the old stories and the laws say?"

"Love God most of all, and love others as you love yourself," answered the man.

"You are right," said Jesus. "You know what to do."

"But who are these 'others'?" asked the man.

Jesus told a story.

"Once there was a man who went on a journey.

"On the way, robbers attacked him. They took everything he had and beat him up.

"They left him lying in the road.

"A priest from the Temple came along.

"He saw the man, but hurried on by on the other side of the road.

"A helper from the Temple
came along.

"He came and looked
at the man. Then he
hurried on by.

"A Samaritan came along."

"Samaritans are no good,"
said someone listening. "They
don't like us, and we don't
like them."

Jesus went on with the story:
"The Samaritan saw the
man. He stopped. He
bandaged the man's cuts.

"Then he lifted the man onto
his donkey and took him to
an inn.

"He gave the innkeeper some money. 'Take care of him till I come back,' he said. 'If you need to spend more, I'll pay the extra.'"

Then Jesus asked the teacher a question: "Who showed the right way to love others?"

"The one who was kind," answered the teacher.

Jesus said, "You go, then,
and do the same."

The Lost Sheep

Jesus welcomed all kinds of people: he didn't seem to mind what sort of people they were.

Some had become rich by cheating.

Some lived bad lives.

Some had the kinds of diseases that no one else wanted to get near.

The teachers were surprised. "What sort of person is Jesus if he wants to be friends with them?" they wondered.

Jesus told a story.

"Imagine that you have a
hundred sheep. You take
good care of them.

"One day when you are
counting them, you find
that one is missing.

"Where can it be?
What are you going to do?

207

"You leave the other ninety-nine
nibbling in the pasture.

"You go looking for the
one that is lost.

"You look high…

and low…

and everywhere in between…

"When you find it, you are
so happy you pick it up and
carry it home.

"You call out to your friends,
'Come and celebrate with me!
I had lost this sheep, but I
have found it again!'

"God is like that shepherd," said Jesus.
"God sees the people who live good lives.
God also sees those who have wandered
away from what is good—and God cares
about them too.

"There is more happiness in heaven when one is found and brought back home than over ninety-nine that are already safe."

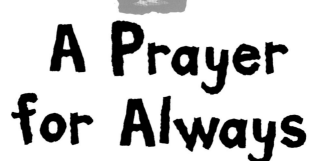

A Prayer
for Always

Jesus liked to pray to God.

Sometimes he went into
a room by himself and
closed the door. There,
alone and quietly, he
prayed to God.

Sometimes he got up early
and went for a walk in the
hills. There, alone and
quietly, he prayed to God.

"Teach us to pray," his
friends asked him.

"Here is a prayer for
always," said Jesus.

"Father in heaven:
May your name be kept holy.
May your Kingdom come
and may your will be done
on earth as it is in heaven."

"I know what that means,"
said one of the friends.
"God is our kind father. We
want people to obey God so
the whole world is as good
as heaven."

"Next," said Jesus, "say this:

"Give us today the food
we need."

"Oh good, I don't like being
hungry," said one.

"Food makes the body strong," said another, "but we also need God to encourage us, to make us strong inside."

That made everyone think.

"Ask God this," said Jesus.

"Forgive us the wrongs we have done, as we forgive the wrongs that others have done to us."

"Do we always have to forgive
everyone?" asked the friend called Peter.
"I try, but some people go on doing bad
things."

"You must forgive everyone over
and over again," said Jesus.

"Then," said Jesus, "say this:

"Do not bring us to hard testing, but
keep us safe from the Evil One."

Everyone looked a bit sad.

"Do hard things happen
to people who live
as God wants?"
someone asked.

Jesus sighed and nodded. He knew
there were hard times ahead.

"But God is God forever and ever,"
another replied.

And that made everyone glad.

Almost
the End

It was a day in spring, on the road to Jerusalem.

Many people were going to celebrate the Passover festival at the Temple there.

Jesus came along, riding on a donkey.

The crowds welcomed him like a king. They waved palm branches and cheered. "This must be the beginning of Jesus making the whole world a better place," they said to each other.

Jesus went to the Temple. It was like a marketplace. People were selling the things people needed to buy for the festival.

Jesus could see that they were
making people pay too much.

Suddenly he began upsetting
the whole market.

"How dare you!" shouted the people in
charge of the Temple.

"The Temple is meant to be a place where you pray," said Jesus. "Not a place where people are cheated."

The people in charge were very angry.

"We must get rid of Jesus," they whispered. They began to make a plan.

A few days later, Jesus met with his
friends to eat the festival meal.

He warned them of hard times ahead.

He told them always to love one
another.

He shared bread and wine with them.
He told them always to share bread
and wine and to remember him in
this special way.

Then Jesus went out to
a quiet place to pray.

"Father God," he said,
"I don't want these hard
times, but I will do what
you want."

Already one of Jesus' friends
had joined the plan to get rid
of Jesus.

He came with soldiers who
took Jesus away.

The next day, Jesus
was put to death,
nailed to a cross of
wood.

In the evening, a few friends came
and took the body to a tomb.

"We must say goodbye," said one.

The sky was getting dark. "This
must be the end of Jesus making the
world a better place," they wept.

Good News

It was the weekly day of
rest. Jesus' friends were very
sad, for Jesus was dead.

"We'll have to hide," said some. "We might get into trouble for being his friends."

"But we will go back to the tomb," said the women, "to say goodbye properly."

The next morning, very early, the women went. To their surprise, the tomb was open.

Inside were two angels in shining white clothes. "Jesus is not here," they said. "He is alive."

They ran to tell the others, but
no one really believed them.

That evening, two of Jesus' friends left Jerusalem for home. A man was going the same way. As they walked, they talked about Jesus.

"Stay with us," said the two friends when they reached home.

When they began the meal, the man said the mealtime prayer and broke the bread to share it.

The two friends gasped. It was Jesus.
But all at once he was gone.

Other friends saw Jesus.

He shared a meal with them.

He helped them understand
that God is a friend when
people face hard times, and
that God can make everything
good and right again.

He gave them a job to do—to
tell this news to all the world.

Soon after, Jesus went to heaven.

But God gave his friends the help they needed.

They suddenly felt brave.
They knew what to say.

They began to speak to
anyone who would listen.

"Jesus came to us from God," they explained.

"He came to tell us how much God loves us. People tried to stop him, but their plan hasn't worked.

"Jesus is alive, proving that his message is true: God wants everyone to give up bad ways and come home to a place of goodness. God welcomes us all as friends.

"That's everyone in the
whole wide world forever."

The news has been
spreading ever since.

Index

When you look up the pages in this list, remember
to read the whole story to find out more.